GHOST WALK

GHOST WALK

Anton Pooles

Mansfield Press

Library and Archives Canada Cataloguing in Publication

Title: Ghost walk / Anton Pooles.
Names: Pooles, Anton, author.
Description: Poems.
Identifiers: Canadiana 20220443092 | ISBN 9781771262842 (softcover)
Classification: LCC PS8631.O6376 G56 2022 | DDC C811/.6—dc23

Edited for the press by: Jim Johnstone
Typesetting and design: Denis De Klerck
Author Photo: Arman Bahreini

The publication of *Ghost Walk* has been generously supported by
the Canada Council for the Arts and the Ontario Arts Council.

Mansfield Press Inc.
25 Mansfield Avenue, Toronto, Ontario, Canada M6J 2A9
Publisher: Denis De Klerck
www.mansfieldpress.net

Our endings rarely square with our beginnings
—Sir Gawain and the Green Knight

TABLE OF CONTENTS

ANTLERS

Everyone wants wings. Give me antlers, like elk.
Not the fur or the tough hide, just give me antlers and the call.
Follow the elk's bugle through twisted halls of dirt
and you'll know I am king by my antlered crown.

FATHER, GHOST, MONKEY

You bamboozled me into thinking I was born animal.
No one I know now knew me then
and so, cannot tell if this is true or false.

You're deep in the jungle and you're not coming back—
your black coat makes you just another shadow
racing through the high branches.

A KUROSAWA DREAM

after Dreams (1990)

Mountains are rage.
Snow, jealousy.

Don't fall asleep—
they'll lay the quilt on you.

AFTER THE BURNING OF THE APIARY

Bees sound like hail against the windows,

    walls and roof.

        They are in search
of shelter,

     not sweetness,

          and are willing
   to crack open

    skulls to get at it.

After the storm subsides

     I go out with a snow shovel

   to clear the driveway.

PAPER BIRDS
for Bronwyn

Paper grackle
Paper starling
Paper dove
Paper sparrow

Paper robin
Paper crow
Paper swan
Paper owl

~

Paper birds can't fly without help.
Do you take them with you
or leave them hanging in the branches
to become homes for insects?

KING
 after King Kong (1933)

You wear no crown.
The tower, which you rule,
was not built for you.

Beauty screams in your wake.
Splendid, primordial majesty.

The birds of prey
that inhabit this Island
kill from a distance.

ART WITH ASHES
for Spring Hurlbut

I.

Spring makes you the moon—
the eye of the gallery wall.
I stop to admire what you've become,
but feel uneasy—*Look away. Look away.*

2.

Spring makes you airborne—
smoke from a newly vanished flame
or morning fog? I enter.
I am lost in you.

BLUE JAY

A splash of blue amid the rubble
of wooden planks and rusty nails
like an underground lake
not yet seen by the naked eye.
Dive in, feel the sting of cold water.
There are no etchings on the walls,
no history revealed.

DOVE

in the middle of the road.
Feathers floating midair
like pipe smoke. I pluck
a quill—dip it in her blood.
I write "Do not Disturb,"
in the middle of the road.

I LEFT THE ORPHANAGE

Everyone had disappeared.
So, that night I raced down the hill

and into the blackened ravine
where I found a glade of grey flowers.

I wandered in but stopped dead
when I felt the flowers squirm

beneath my feet. They looked up
at me with forlorn faces—

familiar faces. Together, they began to cry.

GARDEN OF EDEN
after Minari (2020)

Father builds a church
out in the empty field—

pews of Korean radish
and Napa cabbage;

stained glass windows
of thinly sliced lotus root.

With an ear pressed against
tilled earth
he awaits water's answer.

THE OLD BLIND GUITARIST
after the painting by Pablo Picasso

plays as green clouds fill the sky.
He plays as bullfrogs croak,
as crickets chirp, as drunk men
return home from the bar
after a hard day's work.

Each string feels like barbed wire,
each note like a thunderstorm
far out at sea. He plays through
the evening, through the stinging
pain of his fingers and back.

He plays as he drifts off to sleep.

THE UNNAMED CREATURE FROM MY DREAM

For three nights I walked the crimson path he bled out,
battling the same lonely prairie. To this day
I'm not sure what he was. Bear, perhaps,
but with thick purple-black fur, the horns of a water buffalo
and eyes that shone like the stars above us.
Tell me, where are you going with that raw red hole
in your chest? You move so stubbornly forward—
that way is just more prairie.

LEVIATHAN

Most run for shelter at the first sign of its approach, but not us—at least not this time. Years of sensing it and now we want a glimpse of its lightning, its rainbow scales. Safe under the plastic bridge in the park we watch it shake Heaven empty. Water rises like Noah's great flood. The plastic bridge becomes a boat.

MONSTER 36
after a klecksograph by Justinus Kerner

Every day he sprinkles ink onto paper—
folds it, unfolds it and creates some sort
of terrible, beautiful creature:
an emperor moth with eyes set on its wings
or the ghost of his mother who died
forty years ago. But, of all his creations
I keep turning to the monster on page 36.
He is crying. I don't know why this is.

WHAT LIVES BENEATH THE PORCH

Knock. Knock.

Something follows as I pace back and forth.

Nails rustling against wood
or the sound of an ancient language?

It wants out but I can't remember
the ritual words:

> *Ph'nglui—R'lyeh—*
> something, something.

Put your tongue to the roof
of your mouth,
cough out its name in two syllables.

What will emerge?

Rodent? Cosmic God?

Knock. Knock.

A great evil
destroying the house under its mighty foot.

MERRY-GO-RABBIT
for Ron Waddling

It was my favourite—why? Perhaps it was the only different choice among the ponies, or maybe it was all that was left available, and I had to like it. The carousel was the brightest spot on earth—a fixed point for an astronaut's eye—a maelstrom of stars with a rabbit shaped moon. Time has since separated the rabbit from its axis. It fell to earth in a fiery mass—landed in the field outside my house. I watched the rabbit burn out, turn cold.

TERRIER

Brandy was his name and colour.
Brandy like your father drank.
Brandy ran fiery, burning, clearing his throat, barking.
Drunk racing in the backyard with Brandy.
Man and beast on the rocks.
I could never tell who was who.

GARDEN OF DEATH
after the painting by Hugo Simberg

Three malnourished men
dressed in black
present me

with a bouquet of lilies
that hang
like church bells

cut fresh from a garden
where the sun never sets—
their polite smiles

chime in me with peace

THE SEA

She placed the note on the kitchen counter and opened the
blue-glass window to let sea air fill the room. Her blue dress
trapped the wind and she sailed down from where her hill
house stood like a weathervane. Down from the hills and the
winds and everything else that rises, down to the shore where
the lighthouse's ray spins like a doll in a music-box. Down
there she dances slowly.

THE WAY DOWN TO THE LAKE

has no obstacles except for five
bone-white trees reaching out
from the cold ground like fingers.

MAY DAY
after Midsommar (2018)

Pass your scream
from mouth to mouth.

Flowers sprout from the crown
like little fires—
bright enough to scorch skin,
to burn grief down to ash.

Lay in the rubble and watch
grief's black smoke
rise and vanish.

OWL

What did you do with the knowledge
Athena whispered in your ear?

Did you relay it to sleeping children
who would one day make good use of it?

Did you share it with your owl brethren,
trusting only those close to you?

Did you keep it to yourself in fear
it would be misunderstood?

Or did you whisper it back to Athena
when she began to turn cruel and unwise?

WISHING WELLS

I am trying to wrap my head around why
anyone would sit at the bottom of a well.

Deities are down there with pails
to catch pennies imbued with wishes.

The worst sensation in the world
is having wet sneakers.

GREEN MAN

I wish I had your lagoon eyes. Not as my own,
but watching from the deep,

where your fingers grow and coil.

I wish I had your fiery tongue. Not as my own,
but flooding my thirsty ear.

FISHEYE LENS

I ate the eye of a fish once.
Now the fish sees through me.

Has it become more human
or have I become more fish?

I close my eyes and hear
the roaring undercurrent.

It rushes in and my heart
pumps it throughout my body.

SANTI'S POEM
after The Devil's Backbone (2001)

Beneath amber water blood rises
from your fractured forehead—red smoke
fills hallways caked in sand.
From the safety of shadows
you watch living visions of yourself
play ball around the bomb
that stands dormant
at the center of the orphanage courtyard—
its violent ghost passed to the man
who brought you
to this *low, dark edge of life.*

NOT YOURS TO TAKE

Cicadas score
the height of summer.

A dog ventures in
after some poor creature—

returns with a bone.

Give it back, give it back
says the field

as it burns nothing
and moves nowhere.

GOYA AFTER DINNER

I.

Again, Saturn has begun eating without him.
Eyes full of panic. Black lips, rotten teeth
frantically gnawing at his son's bloody elbow.

"I don't want to die," the Titan chants
between bites, *"I don't want to die!"*

With his appetite lost
Goya puts down his knife and fork,
blows out the candle, leaves the table.

I don't want to die!

Goya can hear (in his mind)
teeth grinding against bone,
the drip of blood falling to the floor.

I don't want to die!

2.

Goya lives alone in an old house (*I don't want to die!*) where he's ignored
his mother warnings (*I don't want to die!*) about painting on the walls.
He walks the dark hallways past witches and devils; French soldiers with
rifles aimed at Spanish civilians; his lover in black; a burial mound.

I don't want to die!

I don't want to die!

In the dark Goya mutters
the names of his dead children.

I don't want to die!

In his dreams he sees his last
surviving son (*I don't want to die!*)
standing above him (*I don't want to die!*)
holding a large knife. *I don't want to die!*

The hands of children reach out through his stomach.
Saturn died screaming—but Goya is very still
beneath his covers, almost peaceful, watching the firelight
descend from the ceiling to lay flat upon the floor.

A STREET PERFORMER IN TUSCANY

creates wind by playing
a common hand saw with a violin bow.

By the looks of his roots he has been
here a long time;

> face, rain worn;
> hair, tangled wisteria.

A watering can fills with euros
from passing tourists.

Should he ever stop playing, the wind
would stop. The heat

would become unbearable.
We'd all erupt into flames.

IMPALED

Tonight, the sky sops up blood with used cotton balls.
The nine green spikes that protrude from below my window
have pierced it so deeply that it may never recover.

LE STRYGE

Why not follow the Vampire's lead?
Stick out your tongue,
mock the entire city with a disengaged slump.
He knows there's something behind the sun,
but stone wings won't take to the air.

THE CALLIGRAPHY OF "LADY SNOWBLOOD"
after Lady Snowblood (1973)

White awaits colour—
she adds red.

Spring takes it away.

ANT MAN

I once housed hundreds.

Every part of me had a use;
my brain a storage room,
my eyes watchtowers,
my heart a palace for the queen.

But the ants have since vanished
leaving only empty pockets
where nests once were.

ANOTHER KUROSAWA DREAM
after Dreams (1990)

I knock red sand from the bottom of my boots,
cough out black ash.

I'm followed by the dead who don't know
they're dead.

       I tell them one by one.

They toss their eyes into the river,
hang their voices in a nearby tree,

       retire to the passing breeze.

MOTH MAN

My grandfather
collected butterflies.

He kept them in oak boxes,
on a green wall.

I asked him why,
once, and he said:

*They're magicians,
in love with illusion.*

Prove it.

He spread the wings
of the dead leaf butterfly.

*Can you see the sunrise
over the ocean?*

No.

*Then you have
a moth's heart.*

GOLEM

I awoke with stones all over.
Head to toe stones.

My arms stones,
my legs stones,
my brain a stone,
my heart a stone.

The skies immense weight
pins me to my bed.

NIGHT ANXIETY

A slow purr
fills the bedroom.

It's the black cat again—
milky eyes
blinking like muted,
toothless mouths.

Soon a scream expands
until my chest bursts
open with a car tire *pop!*

Mice scurry
out of me.

The cat feeds.

SOMNAMBULIST
after The Cabinet of Dr. Caligari (1920)

Dislodged from the cabinet
I dance upon the world's unbalanced surfaces.

Above, spotlights hiss
like a chorus of fork-tongued devils.

This act is a vaudevillian dream
dead upon arrival—
the audience is not laughing,
they're not even amused.

They riot outside my cabinet door
with torches and pitchforks.

FOG

Voices cut through what eyes cannot.
Can I hear you somewhere in the distance;
elk's bugle, raven's caw?

Unable to see past my nose,
my hearing is attuned
to the fog and it's in pain—

the sun is burning holes through it.

GOD OF

A graveyard of paper tombstones
is laid out on the campus grounds.

I wander through, the bones
of Zeus below my feet;

the antlers of Cernunnos hanging
like a funeral wreath in a nearby tree.

I pass an old man in the isle marked "F-G."
He leaves a half-empty wine bottle at Freya's grave.

A Cry Through Nature

Van Gogh made the cries of crows eternal
like his own cry which passes through nature.
Edvard Munch heard it that evening
when he was out walking with friends
on the outskirts of Oslo. It passed his ear
like a swift black bird and dove into the black-
ened fjord below. Van Gogh stole the red
from Munch's face, brushed it across the clouds.

BLACK FABRIC

I.

In the far, dark
corner of the gallery

I discover
discoloured portraits
where

mothers are cloth
covered altars

for starry-eyed
children.

2.

I dreamt that night
I was in the studio.

Lights blinding.

You
(concealed in black fabric)
held me so tightly
I could scarcely breathe.

3.

A voice from the dark
beyond the lights
tells me to smile—

Click!

I go starry-eyed.
You go into the night,

into dream and poem.

4.

I dreamt that night
I was in the gallery.

Eye to eye
with my younger self

sat upon the forgotten
alter of that ghost.

MORE BONES

I bought them in bulk at Costco.

Sharpen your knife—carve me
a spoon and bowl, a picture frame and comb.

You say it's cheaper to find bones in the ground,
but this way I don't have to polish them myself.

When I've finished the last touches
to our fence of arms,

let's take a drive through the white hills.

LOSE THIS SKIN
after Under the Skin (2013)

The Visitor slips into her most seductive outfit.

                                        Skintight.

Cold water dripping from the ceiling
and far off; Glasgow hums neon sign lullabies.

Lips hunt for lips,   fingers for zippers.

The song from the pub plays on repeat in my head.

What's it like to be so free
So free it looks like lost to me

TO GRAFFITI IN THE ALLEYWAY NEAR WHERE I LIVE

The speech bubble reads: *I want to be someone's favourite.*

I take a closer look,
then back away.

The speech bubble reads: *I want to be someone—*

Every day I pass the alleyway
you are little less.

I want to be—
I want to—
I want—
I—

There's nothing I can do
to prolong your being here.

WHAT I AM

I do not sleep, but I pass through
the hallways of the orphanage
like a soundless dream.
When the moonlight
shines bright, a child will think
he has seen my shadow
against the wall or my face
projected upon the window,
and maybe, he has.
I am as much a part of the orphanage
as the brick and the glass.

THE CROUCHING BEGGAR
after the painting by Pablo Picasso

At that moment she was not begging or praying.

Picasso didn't see a difference between begging and praying,
but he knew something about dreaming, suffering.

For the moment she was not suffering, and Picasso painted
what he saw, a woman dreaming.

FEAR NOT

Why do people say I want to live without fear
Do people say I want to live without fear
People say I want to live without fear
Say I want to live without fear
I want to live without fear
Want to live without fear
To live without fear
Live without fear
Without fear
Fear

NOTES

What Lives Beneath the Porch: *"Ph'nglui—R'lyeh—"* is a fragment from a speech from *The Call of Cthulhu* by H.P. Lovecraft.

Santi's Poem: Santi the ghost of a murdered orphan boy and one of the principle characters in *The Devil's Backbone* (2001). *"low, dark edge of life"* is taken from the poem In *Memoriam A.H.H.* by Alfred Lord Tennyson. The poem is also recited in the film.

Goya After Dinner: This poem is based on *Saturn Devouring His Son,* one of fourteen paintings Spanish artist Francisco Goya painted on the walls of his villa during the years 1819 and 1823. Goya had seven children during his life, but only one survived to become an adult.

Le Stryge: The poem is based on one of the grotesques perched atop Notre-Dame Cathedral.

God of: The poem is based on the *Graveyard of the Gods* Project from the University of Wisconsin.

A Cry Through Nature: This poem is based on the paintings *Wheatfield with Crows* by Vincent Van Gogh and *The Scream* by Edvard Munch.

Black Fabric: In Victorian times, in order to get photographs of children, mothers would occasionally be covered in black fabric. This way they could hold the children still, while not taking away focus.

Lose This Skin: The lyrics used in this poem are from the song *Lose This Skin* (1980) by The Clash.

ACKNOWLEDGEMENTS

Versions of these poems have appeared in *Coven Editions, Dream Walking, The Ekphrastic Review, Floodlight Editions, Heavy Feather, Ice-Floe Press, This Magazine, Thorn Literary Journal* and *Train*. My thanks to the editors.

Thank you to my Mum and Dad for their endless support and love.

Thank you to Jim Johnstone for editing and shaping this book, and for the chapbook *Monster 36* (Anstruther Press) where some of these poems first appeared. Thank you for always seeing the magic in my work.

Thank you to Denis De Klerck and the entire Mansfield Press team for the phenomenal work they do.

Thank you to Catherine Graham for the years of guidance and friendship.

Thank you to Lee Gowan, Mary Komech, Jeff Latosik, David Ly, Khashayar Mohammadi and Samuel Strathman for their valuable feedback on many of these poems.

Anton Pooles was born in Novosibirsk, Siberia and now lives and writes in Toronto, Ontario, where he edits the poetry journal *Cypress*. He is the author of the chapbook *Monster 36* (Anstruther Press, 2018) and his work has appeared in an array of journals and magazines such as *This Magazine, Icefloe Press* and *Long Con Magazine. Ghost Walk* is his first full-length collection.